EMERGENCY LESSON PLANS

Instant activities to use for any teaching emergency!

Concept: Geoffrey R. Lorenz
Authors: Judy A. Johnson
         Bonnie J. Krueger
Editor: Barbara S. Meeks
Cover and Book Design: Patti Jeffers

Permission to photocopy the student activities in this book is hereby granted to one teacher as part of the purchase price. This permission may only be used to provide copies for this teacher's specific classroom setting. This permission may not be transferred, sold, or given to any additional or subsequent user of this product. Thank you for respecting copyright laws.

© 2009 Lorenz Educational Press,
a Lorenz company, and its licensors. All rights reserved.
Printed in the United States of America

ISBN: 978-1-4291-0393-0

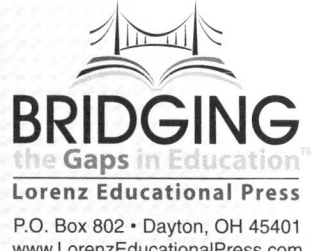

BRIDGING the Gaps in Education™
Lorenz Educational Press
P.O. Box 802 • Dayton, OH 45401
www.LorenzEducationalPress.com

National Education Standards Addressed:

Supports National Standards

Grades 3-4	Animal Training	Bike Riding	Hercules	Ice Cream	Left-handedness	Roller Coasters	Spiders	T. rex
English:								
NL-ENG.K-12.1	X	X	X	X	X	X	X	X
NL-ENG.K-12.3	X	X	X	X	X	X	X	X
NL-ENG.K-12.4	X	X	X	X	X	X	X	X
NL-ENG.K-12.5	X		X	X	X	X	X	
Mathematics:								
NM-PROB.PK-12.2		X	X	X	X	X	X	X
NM-PROB.PK-12.3		X	X	X	X	X	X	X
NM-PROB.CONN.PK-12.3		X	X	X	X	X	X	X
NM-NUM.3-5.1			X		X		X	X
NM-NUM.3-5.2		X	X		X		X	X
NM-NUM.3-5.3		X	X		X		X	X
NM-ALG.3-5.1				X		X		
Science:								
NS.K-4.2						X		
NS.K-4.3	X						X	X
NS.K-4.5				X		X		
Social Studies:								
NSS-G.K-12.1			X			X		
Technology:								
NT.K-12.3	X		X	X	X	X	X	X
NT.K-12.5	X		X	X	X	X	X	X

How to Use This Book

Have you ever wakened in the morning not feeling well? You have a terrible headache or the flu bug that has been going around has finally hit you. It's too late to find someone to take over your class so you HAVE to teach. Or perhaps you are pulled out of class for an unexpected meeting, assembly or conference. To temporarily fill in for you, where can you find simple lessons that are easy to use and take little or no preparation? You need activities that your students will enjoy working on while learning at the same time!

Welcome to *Emergency Lesson Plans*, a collection of educationally-based, cross-curricular activities that are ready to use for any emergency teaching situation. This unique selection of articles and non-fiction stories appropriate for specific grade levels can serve as a starting point for cross-curricular studies. They can also easily be added to existing classroom studies because of the wealth of subjects covered and their support of multiple National Education Standards.

It's always a good idea to have a backup plan, just in case the situation rises. Let these emergency lesson plans help you with those "I just can't teach right now" moments.

Table of Contents

Animals at Work (Animal Training) 4

A Bike Like No Other (Bike Riding) 9

Eek! A Spider! (Spiders) 14

Left is All Right (Left-handedness) 20

The Lizard King (T. rex) 25

Scream Machines (Roller Coasters) 31

The Strongest Man in the World (Hercules) 37

We All Scream for Ice Cream (Ice Cream) 43

Animals at Work

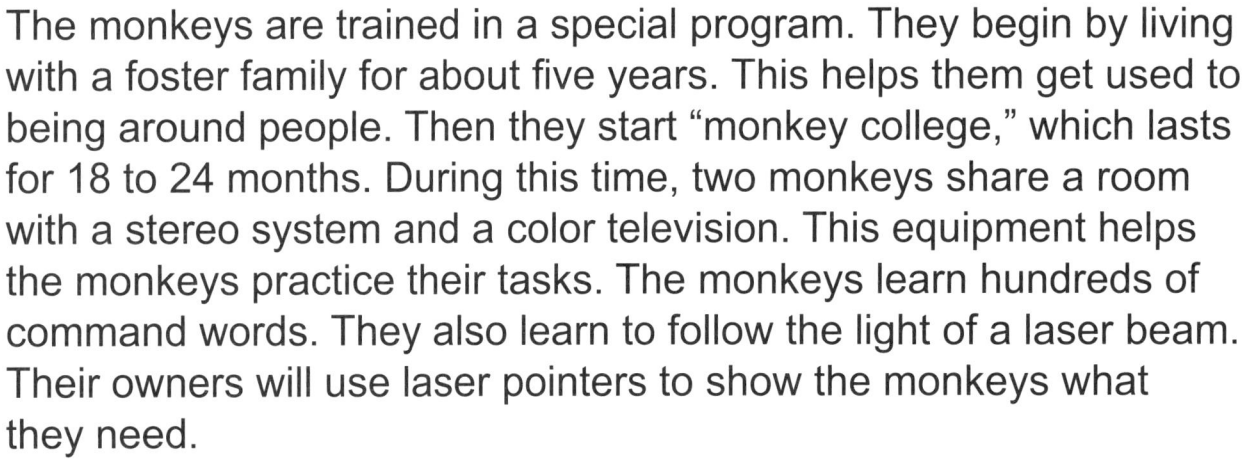

Some animals work every day helping people who are disabled. They offer them the fun of having a pet. They also help people be more independent. Two common animal helpers are monkeys and dogs.

Monkeys have been trained to serve as the hands for people who can't move. These monkeys can turn on light switches or hold books or magazines. They can also use special tools that help people feed themselves.

The monkeys are trained in a special program. They begin by living with a foster family for about five years. This helps them get used to being around people. Then they start "monkey college," which lasts for 18 to 24 months. During this time, two monkeys share a room with a stereo system and a color television. This equipment helps the monkeys practice their tasks. The monkeys learn hundreds of command words. They also learn to follow the light of a laser beam. Their owners will use laser pointers to show the monkeys what they need.

The monkeys are carefully matched with the person they will help. The monkeys may live for 30 or 40 years. Some of the human-monkey teams have worked together for more than 20 years.

Dogs are often used to help visually impaired people. The guide dog movement began in the early 1900s. After World War I ended, the Germans trained dogs to help soldiers who had lost their sight. A magazine article about the guide dogs was published in the United States. Some people who were interested in training guide dogs then began a school.

Animal Training

Volunteers train and love puppies that will become guide dogs. Training for the job begins when the dogs are about 18 months old. It lasts for several months. The dog and its new owner then train together for a few more weeks.

Dogs learn several basic commands, such as right, left, and forward. Dogs are color blind; they can't see the colors of traffic lights. They judge whether it is safe to cross a street by the traffic flow.

Guide dogs usually work for seven or eight years before they "retire." They can then be kept as pets. Most guide dogs live to be 12 or 13 years old.

One estimate is that there are 10,000 guide dogs working in the United States. However, only about 2 percent of visually impaired people have guide dogs.

Maybe when you grow up you will train an animal to help others. It could be a very rewarding task. Imagine how proud you would be when your monkey or puppy graduates!

Name_____   Date_____

 ## Understanding What You Read

Fill in the graphic organizer below with details from the article.

Animal Helpers

Monkeys	Guide Dogs
How they are trained:	How they are trained:
Who they help:	Who they help:
How they help:	How they help:

Vocabulary Builder

A prefix is a word part placed at the front of a word. If you know the meaning of a prefix, you can figure out the meanings of unfamiliar words. Use a dictionary to find the meanings of the prefixes listed below and write the meaning on the line. Then give an example for each word.

1. un- _____

2. im- _____

3. in- _____

4. re- _____

5. dis- _____

Animal Training

Name_____ Date_____

✏️ Tell Your Own Story

Perhaps your pet or another animal has been a big help to you. Write a story about a time when an animal helped you in some way. You can make up the story if you would like. _____

_____

_____

_____

_____

_____

_____

_____

_____

_____

_____

_____

_____

_____

_____

_____

_____

_____

Animal Training

Extension Activities

 ## Branching Out

- Have students work in pairs or groups to design posters highlighting the connection between humans and their animal helpers. Post the artwork in the room.

- Challenge students to create storyboards of situations in which animals and humans work together. The animal should be the "super-hero" of the story.

- At the Web site http://www.helpinghandsmonkeys.org/ you can learn more about the special training program for monkeys.

 ## Answer Key

Understanding What You Read

Monkeys
How they are trained: in monkey college for 18-24 months
Who they help: disabled people by being their hands
How they help: by following commands and laser beams

Guide Dogs
How they are trained: in special schools
Who they help: visually impaired people by being their eyes
How they help: by following commands

Vocabulary Builder

1. not; opposite of; unkind; unlimited
2. not; impossible, impatient
3. not; incomplete, independent
4. again; review, remind
5. not, opposite of; disabled, disagree

A Bike Like No Other

Speeding down the hill, I feel like I'm flying. The best way to spend a warm day is riding my bike. Some people like to walk, some like to drive, but I like riding a bicycle. I'm the fastest bike rider in the world… at least that's what I tell my little brother.

My bike has five speeds. It's colored bright red, just like a fresh strawberry. The seat is black and shaped like a banana. My bike also has a little basket on the back. This is so I can carry things around with me. My parents gave me this bike for my birthday. It was the best birthday present ever!

I ride my bike everywhere. I like to ride around my neighborhood to ask my friends to play. On nice mornings, I ride my bike to school. Now and then, my mom will ask me to ride to the store. She will have me pick up bread or milk for dinner. I'll only go for food I like – no broccoli!

One day the chain on my bike broke. I was riding home from school. I flew over the handlebars and my knees hit the sidewalk. It hurt a lot, but I didn't cry. I walked my bike to my house. My mom cleaned my scraped knees for me. My dad fixed the chain. I did not want to ride this bike anymore. Every time I saw it, I felt afraid. Days went by, and I still wouldn't ride my bike. My friends would come over to ride with me. I told them I didn't want to go. I did not want to hurt myself again.

Bike Riding

The next week I forgot to turn in a homework page at school. I got home and saw that the paper was still in my backpack – oh no! I knew that my teacher would be leaving school very soon. I wouldn't be able to walk back fast enough. My mom wasn't home to drive me. The only thing I could do was to ride my bike. I was scared just getting on to the seat.

I started to shake. Then once I started moving I knew why I loved riding my bike so much. My fear went away. I made it to school just in time to turn in my paper. I am happy that I got back on my bike that day.

The best time on my bike was on our summer trip to Michigan. We stayed on an island where no cars are allowed. People can walk, ride horses… and ride bikes! I was able to ride my bike all over the island. I rode on paths, up and down hills, and even on the beach. I told my mom that one day I would like to live on this island so I could ride my bike every day!

Some people have become famous for riding bikes. Lance Armstrong became a professional cyclist when he was only sixteen years old. He has won the Tour de France (a bike race in Europe) seven times. At the peak of his career, Lance had cancer. He started a group to help other people who are fighting cancer. I consider Lance my hero because he thinks of others and works very hard. One day I hope to be a hero, too – maybe even while riding my bike!

Name_____ Date_____

 ## Understanding What You Read

Circle the best answer to each question below. If you need help, go back and read the story again.

1. What is the name of the bike race Lance Armstrong won seven times?
    a. Super Bowl
    b. Tour de France
    c. Turkey Trot

2. What body part did the bike rider in the story hurt?
    a. face
    b. fingers
    c. knees

3. Where is the island where no cars are allowed?
    a. Michigan
    b. China
    c. Disneyland

 ## Tell Your Own Story

If you could make your own bike, what would it look like? Would it have racing stripes? Would it have flashing lights and bells? Draw a picture of your perfect bike. Write a few words describing your bike.

My Bike

Name_____ Date_____

 ## Figure It Out!

1. A bike rider is riding down the street at 10 m.p.h. (miles her hour). A big downhill slope makes the rider speed up by 5 m.p.h. How fast is the rider going down the hill? _____

2. Sara has just crashed her bike. It costs $5.00 for a new bike chain and $2.00 for a new basket. How much will it cost to fix Sara's bike? _____

3. Jeff has had his bike for 3 weeks. There are 7 days in a week. How many days has Jeff had his bike? _____

4. It is 2:00 P.M. in the afternoon. A friend invites you to his house. It takes 8 minutes to ride your bike to his house. What time will you get there? _____

 ## Word Play

Unscramble each set of letters to make a word from the story.

1. ktebsa _____

2. orest _____

3. eskne _____

4. dlasni _____

Bike Riding

Extension Activities

 ## Branching Out

- Talk about the analogies found in the story. The color of the bike is compared to a strawberry, as is the shape of the seat and a banana. Make sure the students understand that the objects are being compared - the seat is really not a banana. Find other items in the classroom to use to illustrate comparisons.

- Discuss the idea of a hero. What makes a person a hero? Who are some of the students' heroes?

- Many careers involve the use of bicycles – police, mail carriers, etc. Discuss the different careers with the students. For what other jobs would a bike be useful?

 ## Answer Key

Understanding What You Read
1. b
2. c
3. a

Figure It Out!
1. 15 m.p.h.
2. $7.00
3. 21 days
4. 2:08 P.M.

Word Play
1. basket
2. store
3. knees
4. island

Eek! A Spider!

There is a very old story about a girl named Arachne (A-rack-knee). Arachne was very good at weaving. She wove many stunning pieces of cloth. People came from far away to watch her weave. The goddess Athena did not like Arachne. Athena wanted to prove that she was a better weaver than Arachne. The two women had a contest. They wove for a whole day. At the end, Arachne won. But Athena didn't like to lose. She turned the girl into a spider for winning the contest.

This story probably isn't true, but it is a fun way to begin learning about spiders. Spiders have been around since before dinosaurs. There are more than 35,000 kinds of spiders in the world. They are not insects like flies, ants, or beetles. They are in the same group as crabs. Spiders are very important because they eat a lot of bugs. Without spiders, the world would be crawling with too many bugs!

Spiders come in all shapes and sizes. They all have eight legs. Most spiders also have eight eyes. Even though they have so many eyes, most spiders are nearly blind! Spiders have pincers they use to hunt and eat. The body of a spider is like a suit of armor. This suit is called an exoskeleton. Spiders also have special glands on their stomachs. These glands make silk.

Spiders make silk for many things. It is used to make nests for babies and sleeping bags for adult spiders. Some spiders use their silk as a weapon by wrapping it around their prey. Most of the time silk is used to make webs. It takes about an hour for a spider to make a web.

Spiders

Spiders don't stick to their own webs because they have a kind of oil on their legs. It would take a very long time to spin a web if the spider kept sticking to it.

Spiders have many ways of finding food. A jumping spider can leap inches to attack its dinner. This may not seem very far to us, but it's a long jump for a spider. Spitting spiders spit sticky slime on their prey. This knocks the prey over so the spider can catch it. Fishing spiders put their legs in the water to "fish" for food. Some of them can even swim. Most spiders spin webs to catch their food. These webs are made of sticky silk. Flies, bees, and other bugs stick to the web. The webs hold the food until the spider comes to eat it.

Tarantulas are a special kind of spider. These hairy monsters can grow to be bigger than a dinner plate! Tarantulas eat bugs and other spiders. Some of the bigger ones eat frogs and birds. They use their fangs to bite down like a snake. You have to be careful if you pick up a tarantula. They have many hairs on their tummy that can be flicked off. If these hairs hit your skin, they will sting and burn.

Spiders are everywhere. They can be in your backyard or your garage. They are found in countries all over the world. Many people are afraid of these creatures, but most spiders are harmless. The next time you see a spider, think of what it may be doing. Is it looking for dinner? Is it spinning a web? It's amazing what these little beasts can do!

Name_____ Date_____

 ## Understanding What You Read

Decide whether the following statements from the story are true or false. If it is false, change the statement to make it true.

1. All spiders have twelve legs._____

2. Spiders don't stick to their webs because of a kind of oil on their legs. _____

3. There are more than 35,000 kinds of spiders in the world. _____

4. Spiders have special glands on their stomachs that make cotton. _____

 ## Tell Your Own Story

You have discovered a new kind of spider. What will you name it? What does it look like? How does it catch its dinner? Write a few sentences describing your new discovery._____

_____
_____
_____
_____
_____
_____
_____
_____
_____
_____
_____

Spiders

Name_____ Date_____

📖 Vocabulary Builder

Antonyms are words that are opposites. For example, the words "big" and "small" are antonyms. Find antonyms for the following words in the story.

1. **little** is the opposite of _____

2. **few** is the opposite of _____

3. **false** is the opposite of _____

4. **shrinks** is the opposite of _____

❓ Figure It Out!

1. There are 7 spiders in your grandma's basement. How many spider legs are in the basement?_____

2. It takes a certain young spider 2 ½ hours to make a web (he's still learning). How many minutes is this?_____

3. One day, a tarantula ate 5 beetles for breakfast, 3 flies for lunch, and 15 ants for dinner. How many insects did the tarantula eat that day?

   _____

4. Jack the Jumping Spider spun a web that was 2 feet long. Sara the Spitting Spider spun a web that was twice as long as Jack's web. How many inches long was Sara's web? (Hint: there are 12 inches in a foot.) _____

🔤 Word Play

Unscramble the following sets of letters to make a word from the story.

1. hgtie _____

2. ycktis _____

3. mraor _____

4. ratnutlaa _____

Spiders   17

Weaving Through the Web

Help the spider move through the web to find its dinner!

Spiders

Extension Activities

 ## Branching Out

- Read sections of the book, *Charlotte's Web*, by E.B. White to the class. Discuss with the students the positive qualities of spiders. Why are spiders often looked at in such a negative way?

- Have an arts and crafts activity with the class. Make your own spider web or design your own spider. Hang them around the classroom in celebration of these helpful creatures.

- Most spiders are harmless, but a few species found in the U.S. can be dangerous to humans. What species are these? Discuss with the class what kind of first aid is necessary for spider bites.

 ## Check It Out!

- Visit this Animal Planet Web site to watch videos, see pictures, and learn more about all kinds of creepy crawlers. http://animal.discovery.com/guides/atoz/spiders.html

- Tarantulas are some of the biggest and hairiest spiders in the world. Learn more about these oversized creatures at the National Geographic Web site.
http://www.nationalgeographic.com/tarantulas

- Check out the Spider's Parlor in Australia to learn all kinds of fun facts about spiders. They'll even show you how to make your own spider web.
http://www.museum.vic.gov.au/spidersparlour/

 ## Answer Key

Understanding What You Read
1. F – 8 legs
2. T
3. T
4. F – silk

Vocabulary Builder
1. big
2. many
3. true
4. grows

Figure It Out!
1. 56 spider legs
2. 150 minutes
3. 23 insects
4. 48 inches

Word Play
1. eight
2. sticky
3. armor
4. tarantula

Weaving Through the Web

Spiders

Left is All Right

My older brother, Juan, had promised to play catch with me after school. I grabbed my glove and hurried into the back yard.

"Finally," I said with relief, "something is going to be easy today."

"What's the problem, Jorge?" Juan asked, pitching me a curve ball.

"It's been a very right-handed day, so I've been feeling left out," I said, as the ball smacked my glove.

"Ah, don't I know," Juan said sympathetically. "An art project with scissors?"

"Oh, yes," I said, snapping the ball back to him. "Those scissors aren't meant to cut in my hands! Then I smeared ink all over my papers, because my left hand smudged the ink before it dried. When I ran out of paper, I borrowed Rafe's spiral notebook, and those wire spirals really hurt my hand!"

"Not much fun," Juan agreed, tossing the ball back with his left hand.

"Mike and I are the only two lefties in class. Why is it just us guys?" I wondered, chasing after Juan's throw.

"I'm working on a project for biology about handedness," Juan told me, catching the ball I threw. "Only ten to fifteen percent of people are left-handed. More guys than girls are left-handed, too."

"Why is that?"

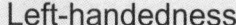
Left-handedness

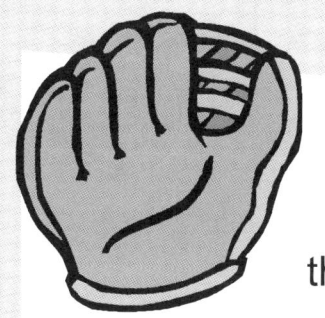

"They don't know. There are all kinds of ideas, but none have been proven. You're in good company, though. Lots of famous people have been left-handed."

"Who?" I asked as the ball landed firmly in my glove.

"Well, several United States presidents, for example. Harry Truman, Gerald Ford, George H. W. Bush, and Bill Clinton were all lefties," Juan replied.

"Really? That's encouraging," I admitted. "If they could sign bills into law with their left hands, maybe there's hope for me."

"Of course there's hope for you. Take baseball. Left-handed pitchers have it easy because they face any runner on first base. Left-handed batters are also two steps closer to first. Babe Ruth, 'Shoeless Joe' Jackson, and Ty Cobb are just three great baseball players who were lefties."

"Many famous artists were also left-handed," Juan went on after catching the ball. "Ever hear of Charlie Chaplin? He was an actor in silent films. Artists like Leonardo da Vinci and Pablo Picasso were also lefties."

"Maybe there are some good things about being left-handed," I admitted. "Thanks for the practice," I said. "I smell something good coming from the kitchen. Maybe Dad's cooking tonight."

"Let's go see," Juan answered. "I'm starving. We can just be glad we don't have to eat with our hands. In some countries, it's rude to eat with your left hand, so it could get messy."

"I think I can manage a right-handed fork tonight," I laughed, as we headed into the house.

Name_____ Date_____

 ## Understanding What You Read

Mark each statement below true or false in the blank provided.

_____ 1. More girls than boys are left-handed.

_____ 2. Left-handers make up about 50% of the population.

_____ 3. Several presidents have been lefties.

_____ 4. Scissors can be used equally well by left-handers and right-handers.

_____ 5. Babe Ruth and Charlie Chaplin were both lefties.

 ## Tell Your Own Story

Have you ever had trouble using a tool or performing a task? Write a funny story about what happened. You can make it up if you'd like. _____

_____
_____
_____
_____
_____
_____
_____
_____
_____

Left-handedness

Name _____ Date _____

 **Vocabulary Builder**

Antonyms are words that are the opposite in meaning to other words. Write an antonym for each word listed below.

1. older _____

2. easy _____

3. famous _____

4. better _____

5. day _____

 **Figure it Out!**

1. Robert Smith Elementary School has 500 students. If lefties make up 10–15% of all people, what would be the least and the greatest number of students who are left-handed?

   Least _____   Greatest _____

2. Smith School has five grades. How many desks for lefties does each grade need?

   Between _____ and _____

Left-handedness

Extension Activities

 ## Branching Out

- Invite students to learn more about a famous left-handed person and to share their findings with the class. You may wish to divide the class into small groups and assign them categories such as sports, politics, sciences, and the arts.

- The Web site http://www.metmuseum.org/special/Leonardo_Master_Draftsman/draftsman_left_essay.asp has an interesting article on daVinci's left-handedness. You may want to encourage young artists to try drawing with their left hands.

- You can take a test to find out your handedness at http://faculty.washington.edu/chudler/rightl.html.

 ## Answer Key

Understanding What You Read

1. F
2. F
3. T
4. F
5. T

Vocabulary Builder

1. younger
2. hard
3. unknown
4. worse
5. night

Figure it Out!

1. Least = 50, Greatest = 75
2. Between 10 and 15

The Lizard King

All through the forest, the ground shakes. It sounds like the footsteps of a giant. Small animals run away at the sound. The giant is getting closer. What could it be?

Out of nowhere comes a loud roar. Something appears through the trees. A large lizard comes into view. It is taller than a giraffe and has a huge head. It's a Tyrannosaurus rex!

The T. rex lived long before humans. They do not live anywhere on earth today. We know about these dinosaurs because of bones found buried in the ground. The first T. rex bones were found in Montana. No one had ever seen dinosaur bones like these before! Henry Osborn was the person who named the Tyrannosaurus rex. This great dinosaur's name means "tyrant lizard king".

The T. rex was a huge animal. Some of them weighed as much as 5 to 7 tons. That is as big as an elephant! These dinosaurs were also very long. The T. rex was as long as two big yellow school buses. The T. rex had a large skull and a huge jaw filled with two rows of sharp teeth. He had to have a very heavy tail to balance the weight of his big, heavy head. Without a tail, the T. rex would fall on his face!

Carnivores are animals that eat meat. The T. rex was one of the largest carnivores to ever live on earth. Having huge, sharp teeth and a strong jaw made killing other dinosaurs very easy. Most animals use their arms and legs to help hunt, but the T. rex had two very short arms. They were like tiny twigs attached to a huge tree. The arms of the T. rex were too short to bring food to his mouth!

Today, the biggest, most complete skeleton of a T. rex is at the Field Museum in Chicago, Ilinois. This T. rex has been nicknamed "Sue" after the woman who found the bones. Sue's teeth are each a foot long!

What happened to the T. rex? No one knows for sure. Some say that a giant rock from space hit the earth. This rock caused thick clouds of dust to block the sun. Without sun, animals could not grow, and carnivores like the T. rex had no food. Some think that changes in the weather led to their death. Maybe an earthquake made all T. rexes fall over – but they couldn't get up because of their tiny arms! We may never know how the dinosaurs died, but we will keep learning all we can about these exciting beasts. Who knows, maybe a new "tyrant lizard king" will appear in the future. But for his sake, let's hope this time he has longer arms!

Name_____ Date_____

 Understanding What You Read

Fill in the blanks with the correct answers from the story.

1. The T. rex was a _____, which means that they ate meat.

2. The first T. rex bones were found in the state of _____.

3. _____ is the name of the biggest, most complete set of T. rex bones ever found.

4. The name Tyrannosaurus rex means "tyrant lizard _____."

Tell Your Own Story

You have just discovered a brand new dinosaur. What will you name it? What does it look like? Draw a picture of your new dinosaur and explain how it got its name.

Name _____   Date _____

 **Vocabulary Builder**

Write down a word from the story that rhymes with each of the following words (some may have more than one answer):

1. **Feet** rhymes with _____

2. **Wizard** rhymes with _____

3. **Mail** rhymes with _____

4. **Snore** rhymes with _____

 **Figure It Out!**

Use your math skills to answer the following questions:

1. The T. rex could weigh up to 7 tons! How many pounds is this? (Hint: 1 ton = 2,000 pounds) _____

2. A T. rex eats a small dinosaur for lunch at 1:30 P.M. He will be hungry again in 4 hours. On the clocks below, draw what time he ate his lunch, and what time he will be hungry again.

3. You and your family decide to go to see Tyrannosaurus Sue at the Field Museum. It costs $5.00 to get in, $2.25 for a snack, and $7.00 for a t-shirt. How much will it cost to spend the day at the museum?

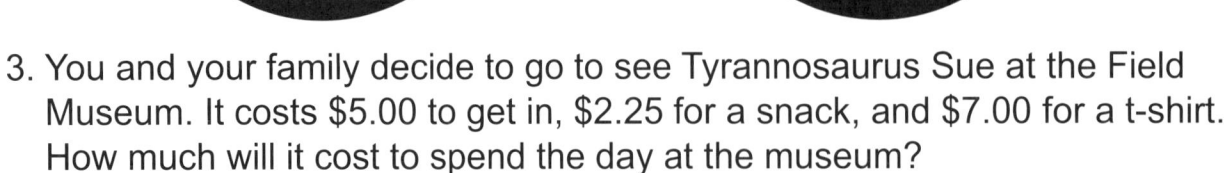

A Prehistoric Puzzle

Use the code below to find the answer to the riddle. Each number in the riddle is replaced by one letter.

What do you call a dinosaur that smashes everything in its path?

A	B	C	D	E	F	G	H	I
11	6	25	10	17	12	4	21	15

J	K	L	M	N	O	P	Q	R
3	26	16	22	2	19	13	7	23

S	T	U	V	W	X	Y	Z
5	9	18	1	24	20	8	14

__ __ __ __ __ __ __ __ __ __ __ __ __
11 9 8 23 11 2 2 19 5 11 18 23 18 5

"__ __ __ __ __ __"!
 24 23 17 25 26 5

T. rex

Extension Activities

 ## Branching Out

- Discuss the difference between carnivores (meat eaters), herbivores (plant eaters), and omnivores (meat and plant eaters). Give examples of each type of dinosaur and the foods they ate. Are the students carnivores or herbivores?

- Certain animals existed in both prehistoric times as well as today (crocodiles, turtles, etc.). Find out what species still exist and discuss these with the class.

 ## Check It Out!

- Today most dinosaur bones are located in museums around the world. The Smithsonian Museum of Natural History has a lot of information online about different kinds of dinosaurs, including the T. rex. Check out the museum's Web site: http://paleobiology.si.edu/dinosaurs

- Do you want to learn more about Tyrannosaurus Sue? Learn where she was discovered and see pictures of her bones at the Field Museum Web site: http://www.fieldmuseum.org/sue/index.html

- Visit Scholastic's Web site on dinosaurs to learn even more about these huge creatures. You can take quizzes, play games, and even build your own dinosaur! http://teacher.scholastic.com/activities/dinosaurs/.

 ## Answer Key

Understanding What You Read
1. carnivore
2. Montana
3. Sue
4. king

Vocabulary Builder
1. meat, eat
2. lizard
3. tail
4. roar

Figure It Out!
1, 14,000 pounds
2. 1:30; 5:30
3. $14.25

A Prehistoric Puzzle
A tyrannosaurus "wrecks"!

T. rex

Scream Machines

"You'll never guess what we're doing in physics class," my older sister, Jennie, said at supper. "We get to design a roller coaster! Once we create our design, we'll make the model of it in class."

"How is that science?" I asked her.

"Well, Andy, we have to know about gravity, energy, and motion to make a fun, safe roller coaster," she told me. "In class today Mr. Banks gave us some roller coaster history. He said they're sometimes called 'scream machines'."

"I've always loved roller coasters," Dad said. "What did you learn?"

"Would you believe the earliest kinds of coasters were built in Russia?" Jennie replied. "They were made out of sleds that ran down human-made hills. People climbed up five flights of stairs to ride for a few seconds. The sleds went about 50 miles an hour. They were called Flying Mountains."

"Well, I know rides today don't last very long," Mom said. "I think they must go faster than that, though."

"Yes," Jennie agreed. "Mr. Banks said there's one coaster that goes about 70 miles an hour. Some drop more than 200 feet."

"Why the big drop?" I asked. "I always feel that I've left my stomach somewhere up in the air."

"The cars of a coaster need to build up energy, so they climb upwards slowly. When the train drops, gravity takes over. The drop gives enough energy to power the whole ride," Jennie explained. "The idea behind roller coasters was used in hauling coal from mines in the 1800s. During the work day, the coal traveled downhill for nine miles, and then mules pulled the empty cars back up the mountain.

Roller Coasters

"Now that's a clever use of gravity," Mom said. "I feel sorry for the mules, though."

"How did the roller coaster make it from coal mining to amusement parks?" I wondered.

"At first, the train rides went slowly so that people could enjoy the scenery," Jennie responded. "The first one went only six miles an hour. It was on Coney Island in New York City. By the late 1800s, roller coaster cars were being pulled to the top of a hill. That first drop added speed and made the ride more exciting. Later, they designed somersault track rides."

"How do they work?" I asked.

"They use something called centrifugal force."

"What? Send who foo force?" I asked.

"Sen. trif. yuh. guhl," Jennie sounded out the syllables for me. "If something is spinning around a center, it's being pushed out from that center."

"I guess once they added loops like that, they had to put in lap bars," Mom observed. "They needed a way to keep customers from falling on their heads."

"Right you are, Mom," Jennie replied. "Higher speed, sharper turns, and centrifugal force all meant new safety rules."

"I know that roller coaster tracks are now made of steel. Are any of the old wooden roller coasters still standing?" Dad wondered.

"The most famous one is at Coney Island," Jennie answered. "It was built in the 1920s and is called the Cyclone. That should give you an idea of how fast it is."

"Hey, I know where we should go on our summer vacation this year," I began.

"I'm way ahead of you, son," Dad smiled. "I think there's a Cyclone in our future!"

Name_____ Date_____

Understanding What You Read

Answer each question below.

1. What scientific principles does a person need to know about to build a roller coaster?
   _____

2. Where were the first "roller coasters" built? _____

3. How was the principle of roller coasters used for work in the 1800s?
   _____

4. When did roller coaster safety features become truly necessary?
   _____

5. What are the newest roller coaster tracks made of? _____

Tell Your Own Story

Have you ever been to an amusement park or special playground? Write a story about what you did there. You could also write a story about a talking animal who rides a roller coaster. _____

_____
_____
_____
_____
_____
_____
_____
_____

Name _____ Date _____

 ## Vocabulary Builder

A synonym is a word that means almost the same thing as another word. You can use synonyms to keep your writing from using the same word over and over. Instead of the word "nice", you could use the words "fine", "kind", or "good". Write a synonym for each word listed below.

1. scream _____

2. hills _____

3. fast _____

4. slow _____

5. push _____

 ## Figure it Out!

Use the following information to create a bar graph on a separate sheet of paper.

The length of a roller coaster is measured by the entire track length used for the complete ride. The numbers below represent the longest roller coasters.

| 8,133 feet | 6,595 feet | 5,600 feet |
| 7,450 feet | 6,072 feet | |

 ## Map Moments

Look at a map of the United States. Some of the coasters with the largest drops are found in the states listed below. Find each state. Which one is nearest to you? Which is the farthest away?

New Jersey   California   Texas

Nevada   Pennsylvania   Ohio

Roller Coasters

Name _____ Date _____

Twists and Turns

Fill in the crossword puzzle using words from the article.

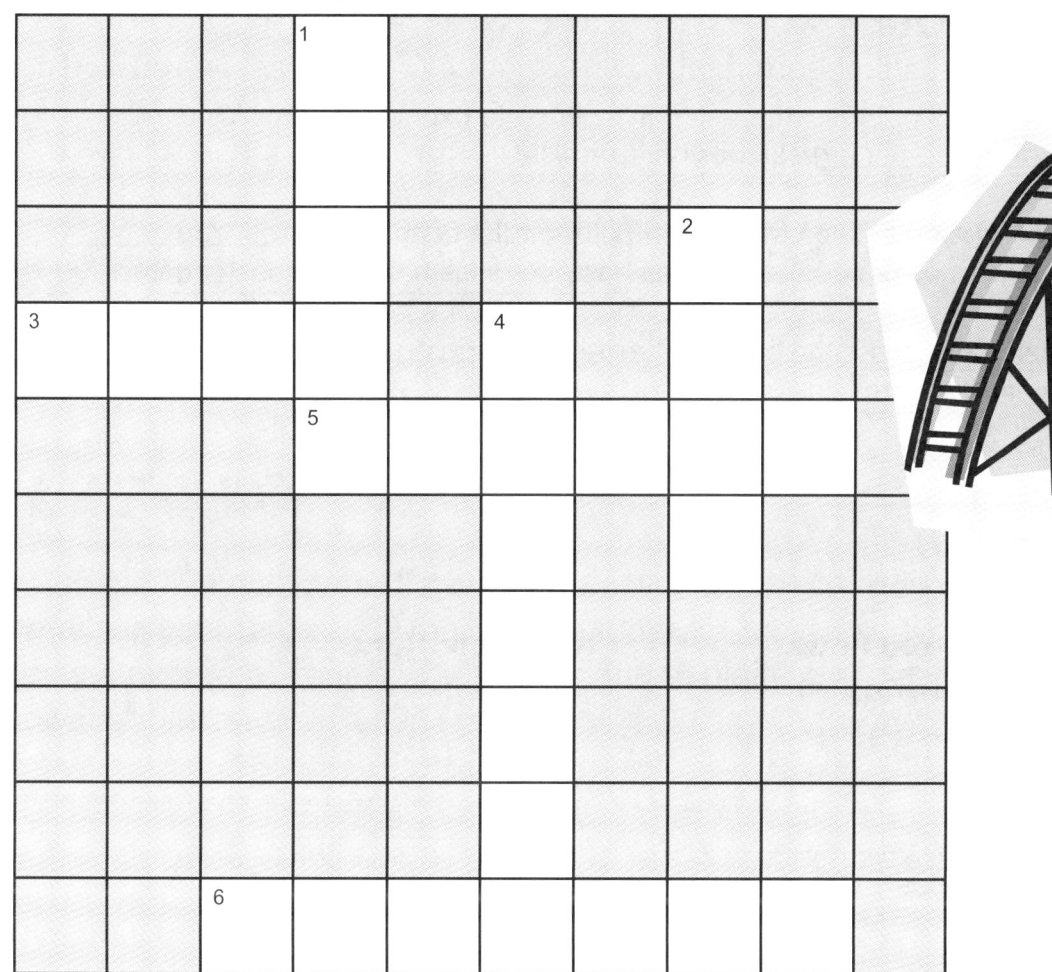

ACROSS

3. The Cyclone at Coney Island is made of this.

5. Roller coasters are sometimes called _____ machines.

6. Coney Island is in _____ _____ City. (2 words)

DOWN

1. The earliest roller coasters were made of _____ running down human-made hills.

2. The idea behind roller coasters was used when moving _____ from mines in the 1800s.

4. This force takes over when the roller coaster drops down a big hill.

Roller Coasters 35

Extension Activities

 ## Branching Out

- Invite advanced students or those interested in science to explore the physics of roller coasters at http://www.learner.org/exhibits/parkphysics/

- Give students practice in creating graphs using other roller coaster records. You can find these records in almanacs or sources such as http://www.ultimaterollercoaster.com.

- You can learn even more about the history of roller coasters at http://search.eb.com/coasters/.

 ## Answer Key

Understanding What You Read

1. Gravity, motion, energy, centrifugal force
2. Russia
3. Coal mining companies used coasters to get coal down the mountain
4. When roller coasters added loops to go upside down and higher speeds
5. Steel

Vocabulary Builder

1. yell, shout
2. slopes, mountains
3. quick, rapid
4. gradual, plodding
5. shove, prod

Twists and Turns

		S					
		L					
		E			C		
W	O	O	D	G	O		
		S	C	R	E	A	M
				A		L	
				V			
				I			
				T			
	N	E	W	Y	O	R	K

Roller Coasters

The Strongest Man in the World

Greece is a nation with a very long history. The people of Greece have always loved to play games and hold contests. Every five years, they had contests to find the strongest men in Greece. These men had to compete in running and jumping. They also had to box and wrestle. The winners of these contests won prizes. They were known as heroes all over the world.

Many myths have been written about these Greek men. A myth is a story that tells about people and places from long ago. These stories may or may not be true – we do not know for sure. One Greek hero found in many myths was named Hercules.

It is said that Hercules was the strongest man on earth. He was the son of Zeus, the king of the Greek gods. A goddess named Hera was jealous of Hercules. When Hercules was a baby, Hera sent two snakes into his crib. When his mother found him, Hercules was holding the snakes and laughing. He was very strong, even as a baby.

Many people in the ancient world had heard stories about Hercules. They thought he could do anything because he was so strong. King Eurystheus decided to test Hercules. This king sent him to do twelve difficult tasks. These tasks would have been impossible for normal men. Was he strong enough to survive the king's tests?

The first and hardest task was to fight a lion. This lion lived in the mountains. The people in the nearby town were afraid to leave their houses for fear of being attacked. It was a huge beast. Weapons could not stop this lion. The bravest men would hide at the sound of its roar.

Hercules arrived in the town and found the lion. He tried shooting arrows at him. The arrows just bounced off. He pulled a tree from the ground and used it as a club. The lion kept fighting back. The hero then wrestled the lion with his bare hands. They fought for very long time. Finally, Hercules won the battle.

Hercules went to the king wearing the skin of the lion. This scared the king. He thought the lion had come to attack him. When the king saw that it was Hercules, he was very angry. Hercules had tricked him! The king made sure the rest of the tests were even harder than the first one.

Hercules had to fight monsters with nine heads. When Hercules cut off one head, two grew back in its place. He fought a dog with three heads. He fought man-eating horses. He even had to clean thousands of cattle stalls in one day.

Hercules finished every task the king gave him. He then went on to have many more adventures. There were so many people to help. It must have been difficult being the strongest man in the world!

Name_____ Date_____

💡 Understanding What You Read

1. Every _____ years, the Greeks held a contest to find the strongest men in Greece.

2. Myth says that _____ was Hercules' father.

3. The first task that the king gave to Hercules was to fight a _____ that lived in the mountains.

4. Hercules tried to beat the lion by pulling a _____ from the ground and using it as a club.

✏️ Tell Your Own Story

Imagine that Hercules lived today. You are a king or queen and want to test Hercules. Write a few sentences telling him what job he must do.

_____
_____
_____
_____
_____
_____
_____
_____
_____
_____
_____
_____

Name _____ Date _____

 **Figure It Out!**

1. Hercules fought a monster with 9 heads. Every time he cut off a head, 2 grew back in its place. If he cuts off 2 of the monster's heads, how many heads does the monster now have? _____

2. It took Hercules 2 ½ days to find the lion in the mountains. How many hours is this? (Hint: There are 24 hours in one day) _____

3. Hercules rescued 19 maidens, 12 children, and 4 men in one day. How many people did he rescue that day? _____

4. One task sent Hercules to another country. He left Greece at 2 o'clock. It took him 4 ½ hours to get to the other country. Show on the first clock what time Hercules left Greece. Show on the second clock what time he got to the other country.

 **Word Play**

Unscramble the following sets of letters to make words from the story.

1. nstorg _____

2. stelwre _____

3. gkree _____

4. knseas _____

Hercules

 # Map Moments

Hercules lived in Greece. He had many adventures in other countries. On the map below, tell which direction Albania, Bulgaria, and Turkey are from Greece.

1. Bulgaria is _____ of Greece.

2. Turkey is _____ of Greece.

3. Albania is _____ of Greece.

Extension Activities

 ## Branching Out

- The Twelve Labors of Hercules is a very popular story in Greek mythology. Tell the stories of the other labors in more detail. Have the students draw pictures of what they think the monsters that Hercules met looked like.

- Hercules' father was said to be Zeus, King of the Gods. Discuss the story of Zeus and the other gods that lived on Mount Olympus.

- What is a myth? Did these stories really happen? Discuss with the class other popular myths in Greek mythology (Medusa, Helen of Troy, etc.).

 ## Check It Out

- Hercules wasn't the only Greek hero who had great adventures. Check out this Web site to read stories about Hercules, Perseus, Jason, and many others. http://www.mythweb.com/heroes/heroes.html

- Do you want to learn more about Greek mythology? This Web site gives information about gods, goddesses, heroes and monsters. http://www.greekmythology.com

- Mythology was only one part of Greek life. Visit this Web site to learn all about Greek art, war, religion, history and more! http://www.historyforkids.org/learn/greeks

 ## Answer Key

Understanding What You Read
1. five
2. Zeus
3. lion
4. tree

Figure It Out!
1. 11 heads
2. 60 hours
3. 35 people
4. 2:00; 6:30

Word Play
1. strong
2. wrestle
3. Greek
4. snakes

Map Moments
1. north
2. east
3. northwest

We All Scream for Ice Cream

There are many interesting twists in the history of ice cream. The early Greeks and Romans flavored clean snow with fruit and juice. In the 1600s, the kings and queens of Europe served ice cream at their royal banquets. George Washington, our first president, enjoyed ice cream. Thomas Jefferson, the third president, even had his own special recipe for vanilla ice cream.

For a long time, only wealthy people could afford to have ice cream. Ice was expensive and hard to get. Inventions such as the icehouse, steam power, electric motors, refrigeration, and packing machines made ice cream affordable for everyone.

People got really creative then! They made ice cream sodas, sundaes, and banana splits. They figured out how to put ice cream on a stick and cover it with chocolate and nuts. They rolled waffle cones to hold the ice cream. Today, an average person eats 21.5 quarts of ice cream a year. People in the United States spend more than $21 billion a year on ice cream products!

So how does the milk go from moo to you? Ice cream makers buy raw milk that has been kept cold. The cold temperatures keep the milk from spoiling. Large refrigerated tank trucks collect the raw milk from dairy farms. Each truck holds about 5,000 gallons of milk. You may have seen a milk truck on the road. It is usually silver and looks like a thermos bottle lying on its side.

At the factory, the milk is mixed with a sweetener such as cane sugar or honey. Other ingredients are added to make the ice cream smooth. Everything is blended in a large tank, and then the mixture is pasteurized. Milk has to go through this process to kill any bacteria that might cause disease. This process is named for the French inventor, Louis Pasteur. He discovered that heating milk kills the germs in it.

The ice cream mix is then frozen. While it is freezing, the mix has to be beaten to turn it into ice cream. Otherwise, the mix would freeze into a giant, flavored milk cube. Large machines have blades that turn in the mix. This churning keeps the ice crystals in the mix from getting too big. It also adds air, which makes the ice cream light and soft. A gallon of ice cream mix generally makes two gallons of ice cream.

After the ice cream leaves the freezer, nuts, fruit, or chocolate chips can be shot or dropped in. The ice cream is then ready to be packaged. It's sent to grocery stores and ice cream shops in freezer trucks.

In 1984, President Ronald Reagan made July National Ice Cream Month. Isn't that a good reason to enjoy the treat, no matter what flavor ice cream you like best? Need another reason? Ice cream has calcium, which everyone needs for strong, healthy bones. That calls for a double-dip cone!

Name_____ Date_____

💡 Understanding What You Read

Place the following steps to make ice cream in the right order. Write the correct number in the blank at the left.

_____ 1. The mix is pasteurized.

_____ 2. Fruits, nuts, or chips are added.

_____ 3. Milk is delivered to the ice cream factory.

_____ 4. The mix is churned in a large machine.

_____ 5. Things are added to the milk to make it smoother.

✏️ Tell Your Own Story

Write a poem to celebrate National Ice Cream Month. Your poem doesn't need to rhyme. _____

_____
_____
_____
_____
_____
_____

📖 Vocabulary Builder

We add prefixes and suffixes to the beginning and ends of words to make new words. Some root words may have both a prefix and a suffix! For each root word below, make as many other words as you can. Try to make at least one using an prefix and one using a suffix.

1. port _____

2. courage _____

3. cover _____

Name _____ Date _____

 **Figure it Out!**

1. Make a circle or bar graph using the following figures about our favorite ice creams. Be sure to title and to label your graph.

Vanilla	26%
Chocolate	12.9%
Neapolitan	4.8%
Strawberry	4.3%
Cookies 'n' Cream	4%
All others	48%

2. Now, make a second graph using the data below on types of ice cream sold. If you made a bar graph for #1, make a circle graph now. If you made a circle graph, make a bar graph now. Give your graph a title and label it.

Regular ice cream	59.9%
Light, lowfat, nonfat	27.8%
Frozen yogurt	4.3%
Sherbet	3.5%
Other	4.5%

Ice Cream

Ice Cream Word Search

Find the story terms hidden in the puzzle below.
The words can be up, down, forward, backward, or diagonal.

```
J  A  S  P  A  S  T  E  U  R  N
I  G  L  U  L  Y  R  I  A  D  W
C  R  N  G  N  C  N  A  G  H  A
E  K  A  I  Z  D  D  M  A  M  F
C  P  N  S  N  C  A  M  R  U  F
R  R  L  U  H  R  I  E  B  I  L
E  N  I  A  V  R  U  T  A  C  E
A  J  J  G  S  V  L  H  G  L  C
M  B  A  N  A  N  A  L  C  A  O
L  F  R  E  E  Z  E  R  P  C  N
Q  S  W  S  I  O  L  C  L  G  E
```

banana   dairy   Pasteur
calcium freezer   sundae
churning ice cream waffle cone

47

Extension Activities

Branching Out

- Have students find out about the importance of calcium and how they can get as much as they need each day. Broaden the topic to include other nutrients. Have students create a healthful eating plan. A good place for them to begin is http://www.kidshealth.org/kid/nutrition/food/minerals.html.

- To see additional ideas for teaching about ice cream (and chocolate!) across the curriculum, check out http://www.yale.edu/ynhti/curriculum/units/1999/4/99.04.05.x.html.

- Have you ever gotten a headache from eating ice cream? If you'd like to know why, go to http://www.kidshealth.org/kid/talk/qa/ice_cream_headache.html.

Answer Key

Understanding What You Read

1. 3
2. 5
3. 1
4. 4
5. 2

Vocabulary Builder

1. export, import, important, supported
2. discourage, encourage, encouragement, courageous
3. discover, uncover, covering, covered

Ice Cream Word Search

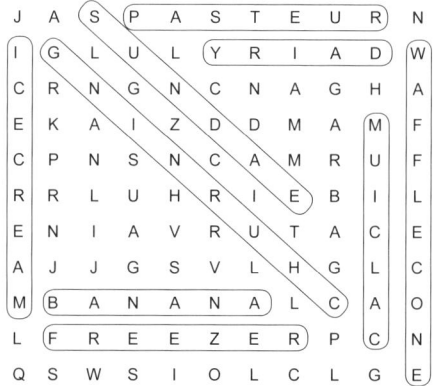

Ice Cream